This Book Belongs To:

_____

Keep Your Fucking Nose Out!

Copyright © 2019 by Cuss Word Gifts

All rights reserved. No part of this book may be reproduced or used in any manner without written permission of the copyright owner except for the use of quotations in a book review.

Fed up dealing with
assholes and bullshit?

Don't bang your head
against the wall,
drink a gallon of wine
or throw yourself on the
floor in a tantrum.

Be like a cat...
just don't give a shit!

OR

Write in this book instead
and soak up some
great motivational quotes
along the way.

Meow........

date: _____   day: m t w t f s s

Asshole of the Day

What I Wish I Had Said

I'm Lucky to Have

MY MOOD TODAY (Rated in cats)

SHIT TO DO

date: _____

SHIT I GOT DONE

PROUD OF

Random Shit

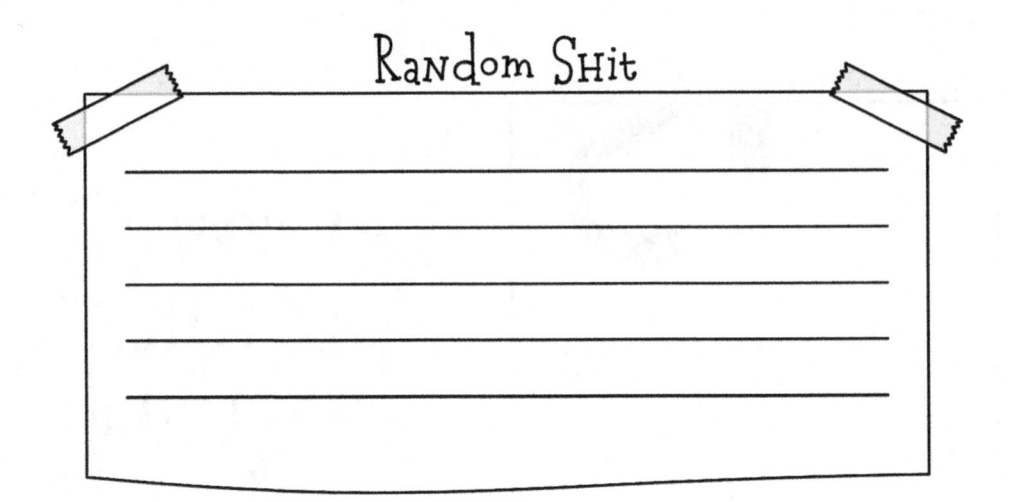

More Random Shit

date: _____   day: m t w t f s s

Shit List of the Day

Other Shit to Remember

CUSS WORDS OF THE DAY

date:_____   day: m t w t f s s

BULLSHIT OF THE DAY

date:_____   day: m t w t f s s

Life is short buy the dress

date: _____   day: m t w t f s s

SHIT I WANT

SHIT I NEED

FUCK FUCK FUCKITY FUCK TO..............

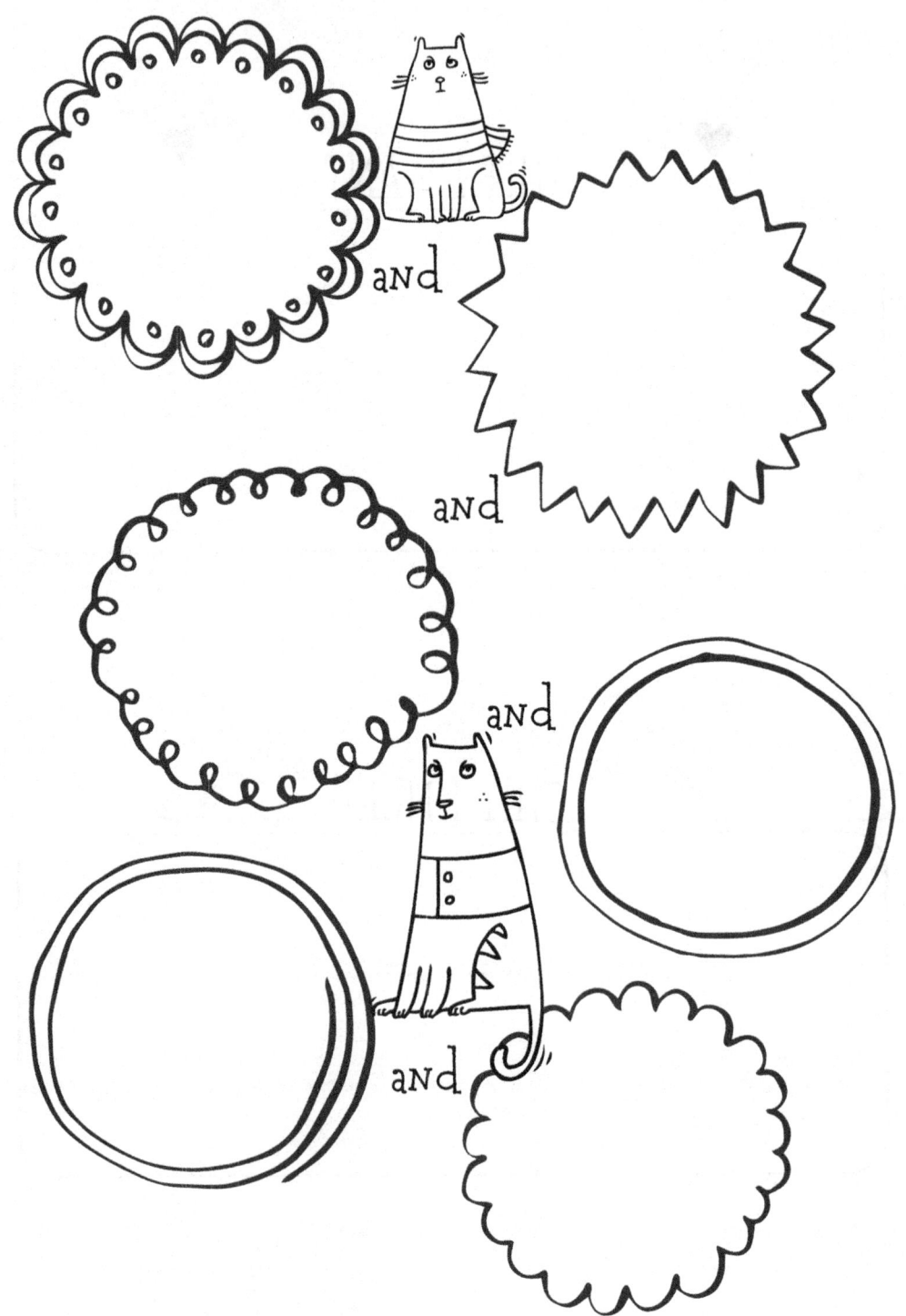

The Greatest Shit I Accomplished This Week

date:_____

date: _____   day: m t w t f s s

Asshole of the Day

What I Wish I Had Said

I'm Lucky to Have

MY MOOD TODAY (Rated in cats)

SHIT TO DO

date: ____________________

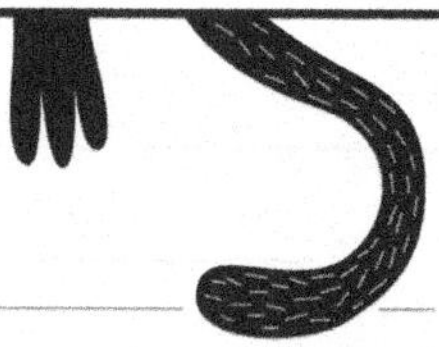

START NOW NOT TOMORROW

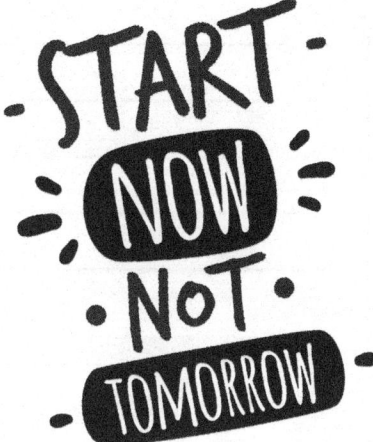

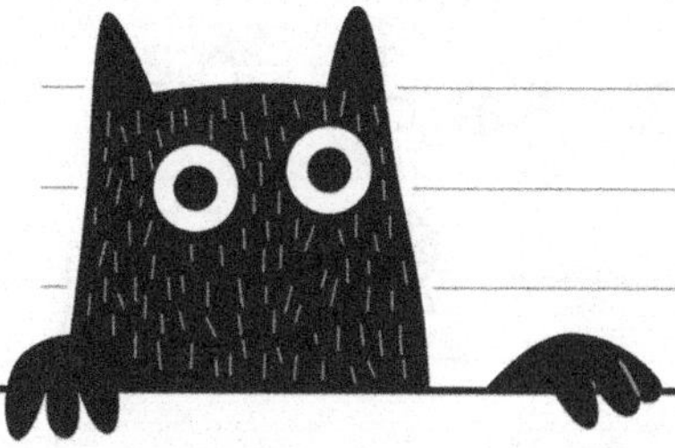

SHIT I GOT DONE

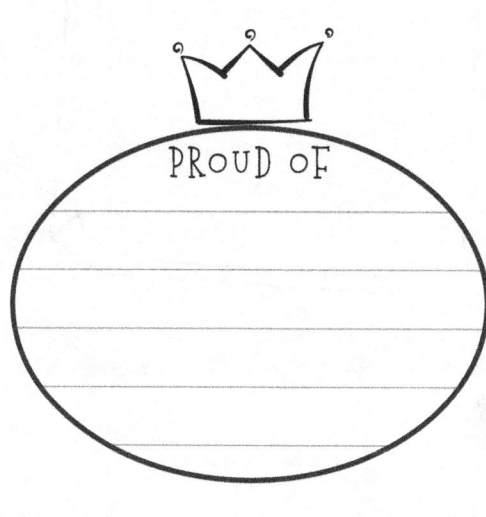

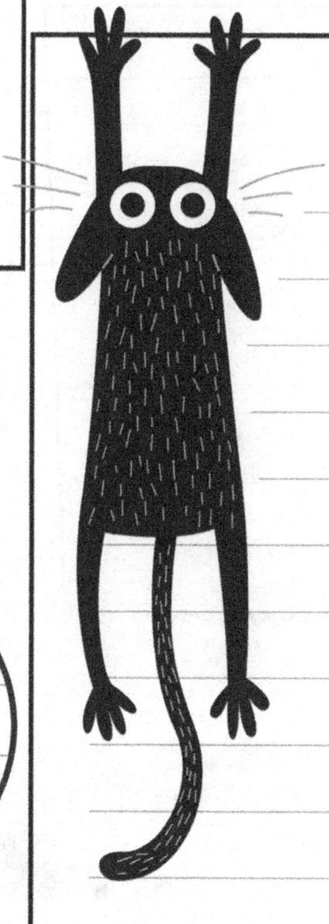

PROUD OF

Random Shit

More Random Shit

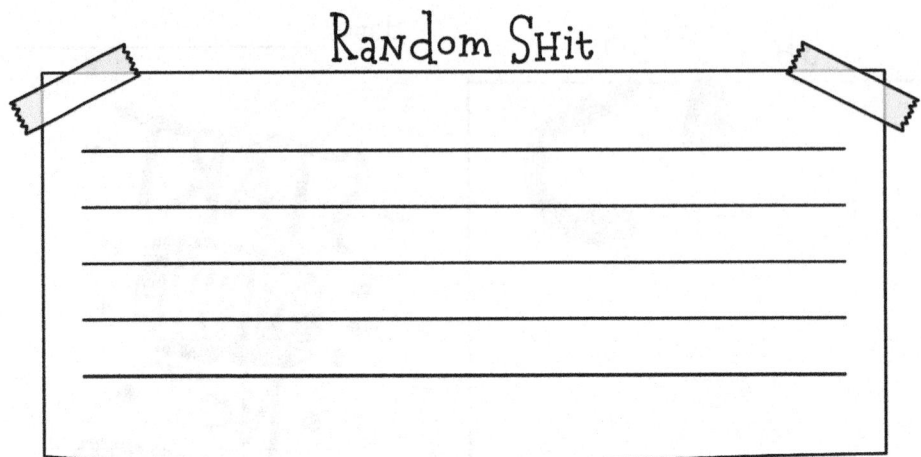

date: _____   day: m t w t f s s

Shit List of the Day

Other Shit to Remember

CUSS WORDS OF THE DAY

date:_____ day: m t w t f s s

coffee FIRST

THEN I'LL DEAL WITH YOUR FUCKING BULLSHIT

BULLSHIT OF THE DAY

date:_____   day: m t w t f s s

date: _____   day: m t w t f s s

FUCK FUCK FUCKITY FUCK TO..............

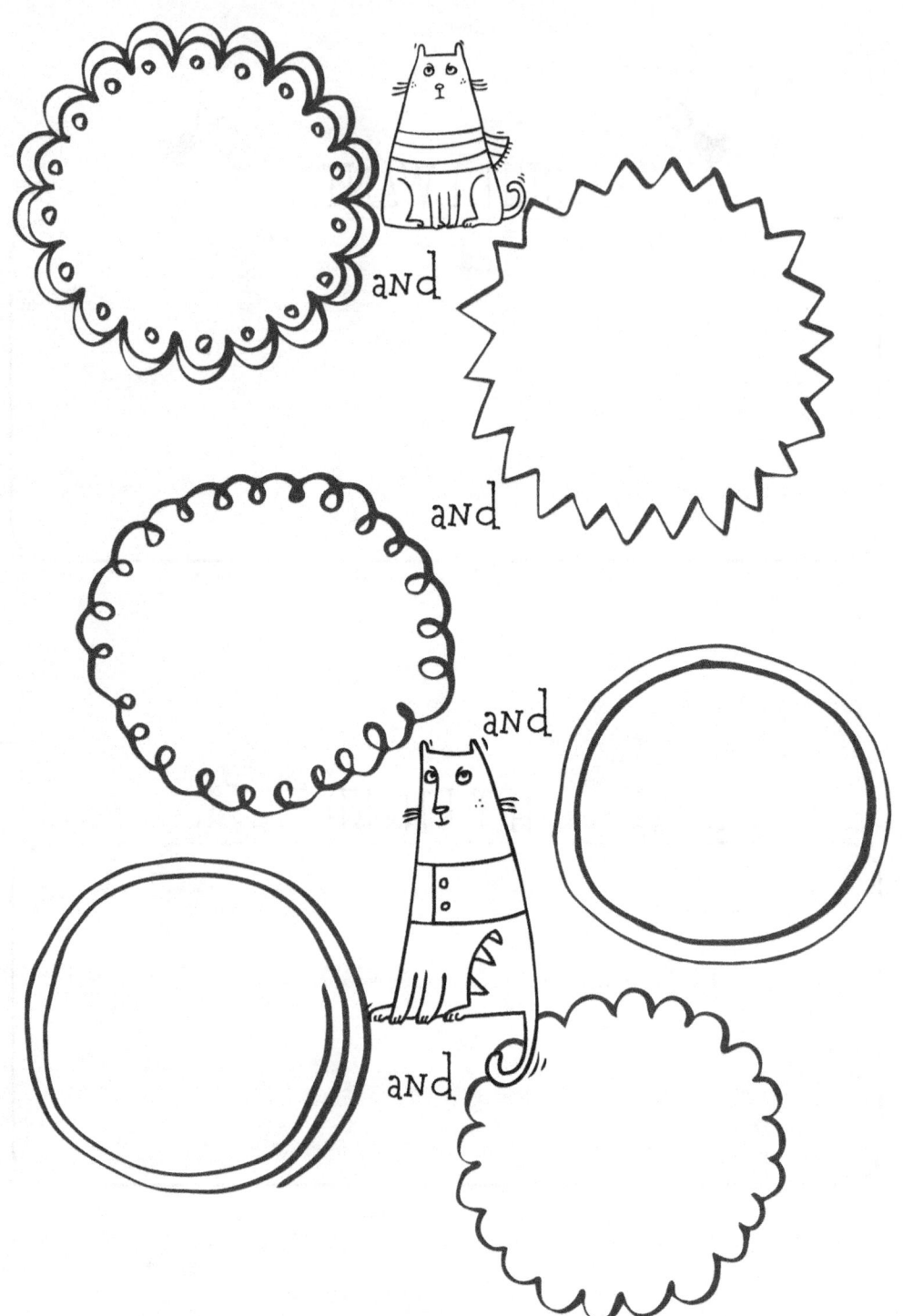

The Greatest Shit I Accomplished This Week

date:_____

date: _____   day: m t w t f s s

Asshole of the Day

What I Wish I Had Said

I'm Lucky to Have

MY MOOD TODAY (Rated in cats)

SHIT TO DO   date: _____

SHIT I GOT DONE

PROUD OF

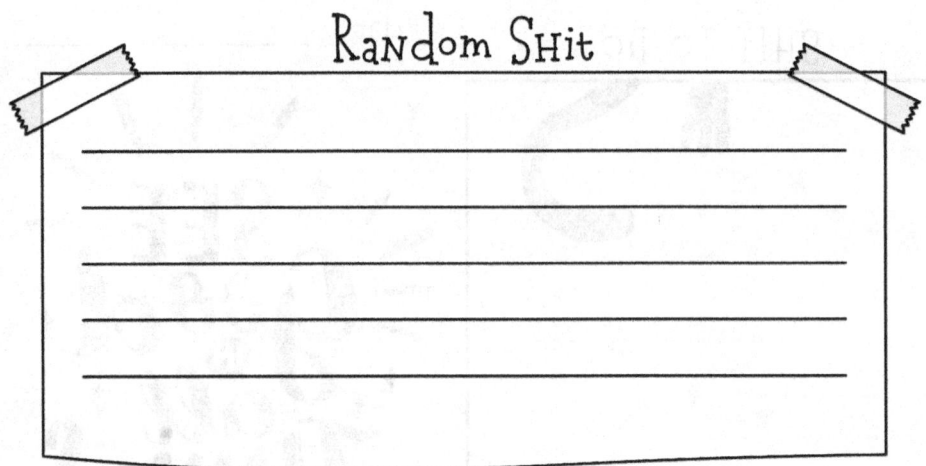
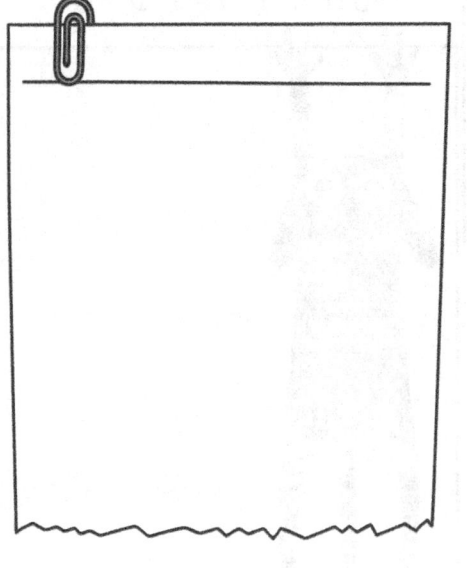

date: _____   day: m t w t f s s

Shit List of the Day

Other Shit to Remember

NORMAL IS FUCKING BORING

CUSS WORDS OF THE DAY

date: _____   day: m t w t f s s

BULLSHIT OF THE DAY

date:_____   day: m t w t f s s

BELIEVE
in yourself
& YOU WILL BE
Unstoppable

date: _____   day: m t w t f s s

SHIT I WANT

SHIT I NEED

FUCK FUCK FUCKITY FUCK TO..............

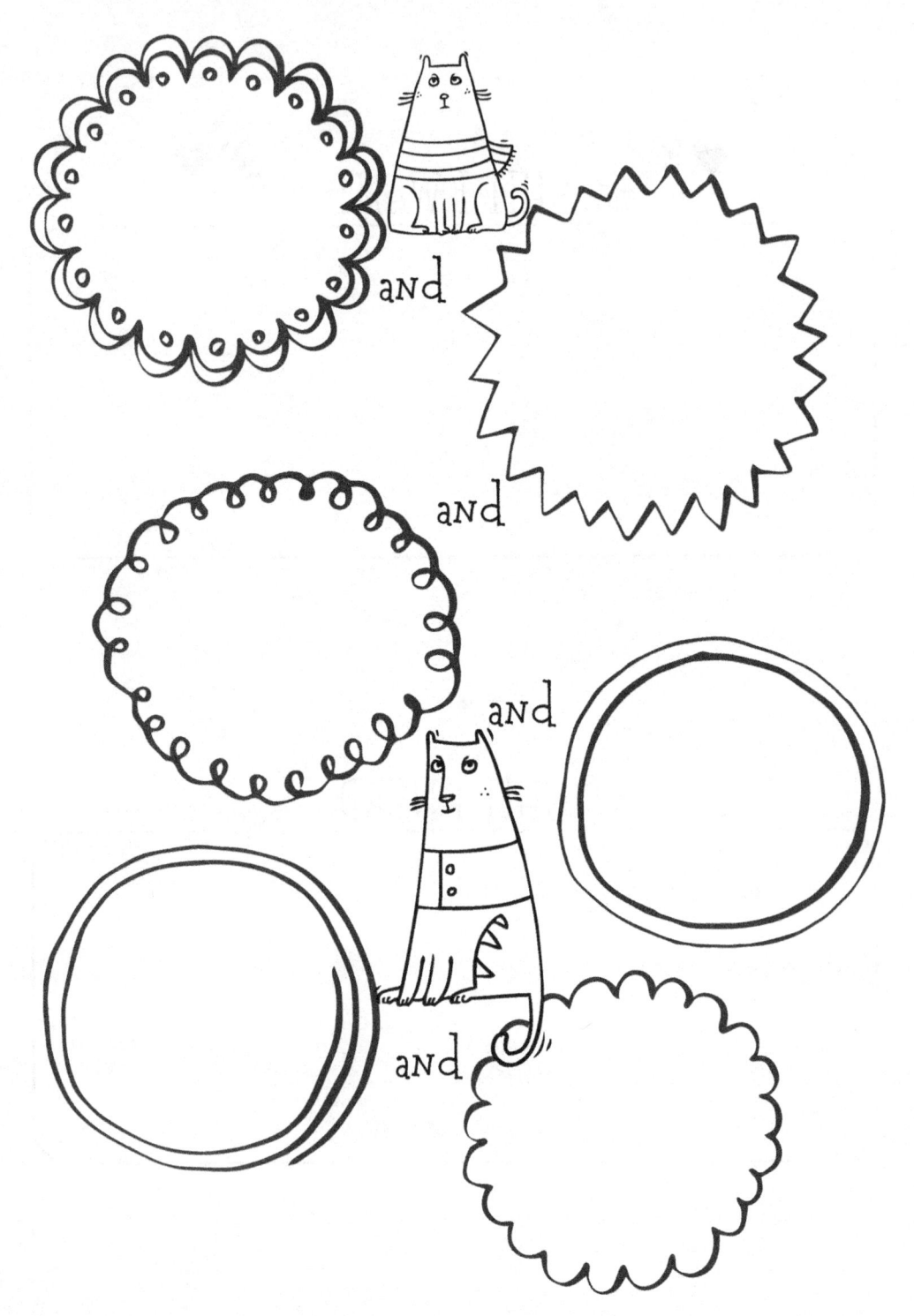

and

and

and

and

The Greatest Shit I Accomplished This Week

date:_____

date: _____ day: m t w t f s s

Asshole of the Day

What I Wish I Had Said

I'm Lucky to Have

MY MOOD TODAY (Rated in cats)

SHIT TO DO

date: _____

> "Do something Creative EVERYDAY"

SHIT I GOT DONE

PROUD OF

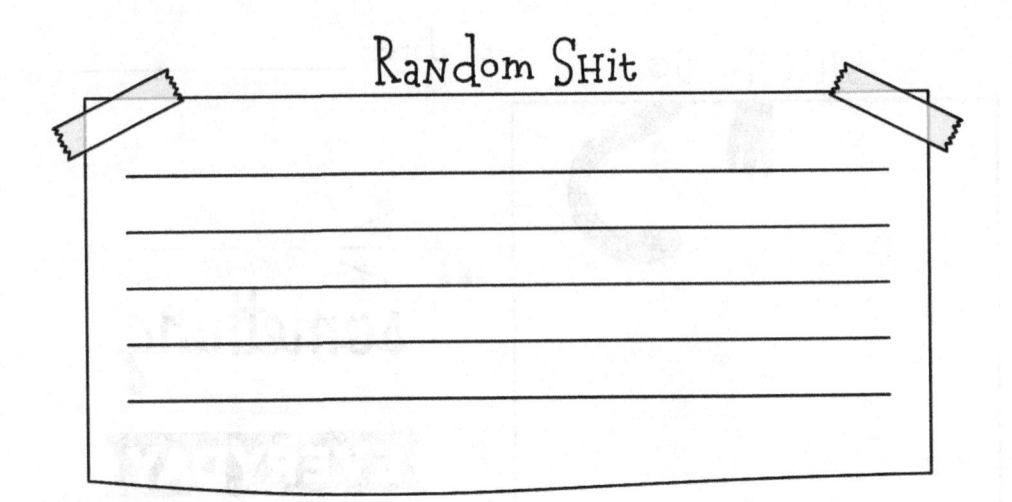

Random Shit

More Random Shit

date: _____   day: m t w t f s s

Shit List of the Day

Other Shit to Remember

I'M NOT Here To Be AVERAGE I'M HERE TO BE AWESOME

CUSS WORDS OF THE DAY

date: _____   day: m t w t f s s

INHALE
THE
GOOD SHIT
EXHALE
THE
BULLSHIT

BULLSHIT oF THE DAY

date:_____   day: m t w t f s s

Work
HARD
Dream
· BIG ·

date:_____   day: m t w t f s s

SHIT I WANT

SHIT I NEED

FUCK FUCK FUCKITY FUCK TO..............

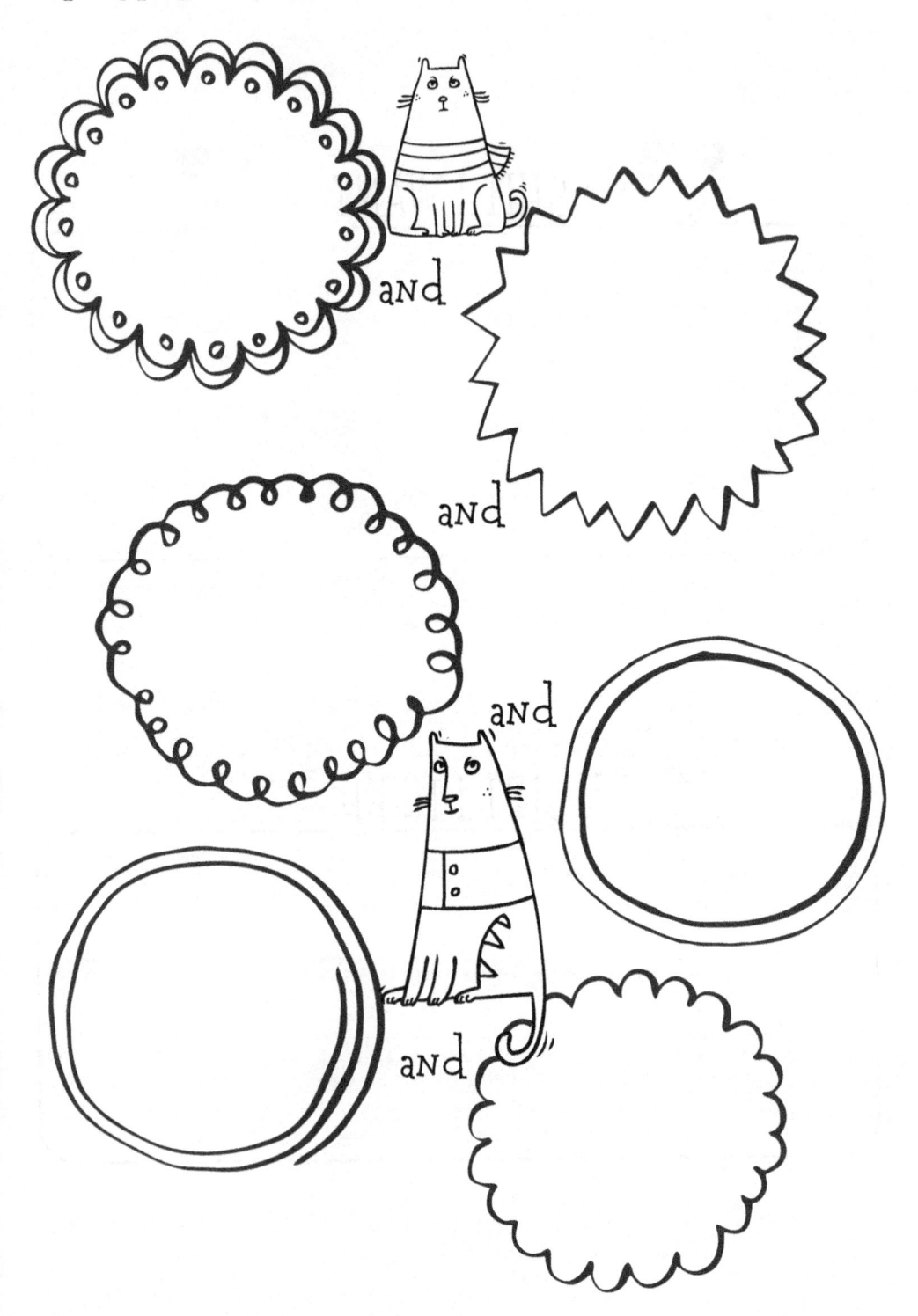

and

and

and

and

The Greatest Shit
I Accomplished This Week

date:_____

ONLY YOU can MAKE IT HAPPEN

SO GET OFF YOUR ASS AND DO SOMETHING!

Currently HAPPENING IN LIFE

MONTH: _____

LOVING	EATING	THINKING
GOING	MAKING	READING
HEARING	BUYING	CELEBRATING
SEEING	DOING	WEARING

date: _____ day: m t w t f s s

Asshole of the Day

What I Wish I Had Said

I'm Lucky to Have

MY MOOD TODAY (Rated in cats)

SHIT TO DO

date: _____

BE your own HERO

SHIT I GOT DONE

PROUD OF

Random Shit

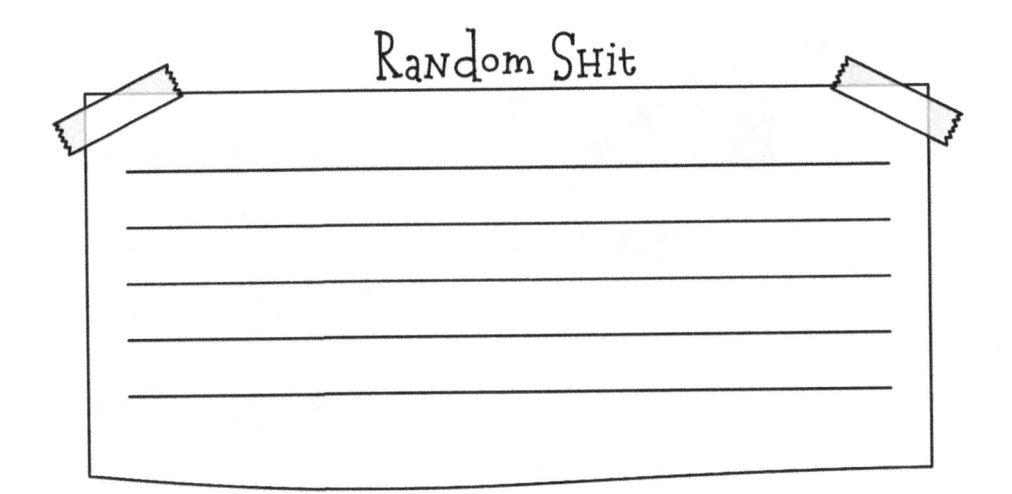

More Random Shit

date:_____   day: m t w t f s s

Shit List of the Day

Other Shit to Remember

Nothing in this WORLD is PERMANENT

CUSS WORDS OF THE DAY

date:_____   day: m t w t f s s

Dear life,

I've had enough fucking bullshit to last quite a while.

Can we take a little break please?!

BULLSHIT OF THE DAY

date:_____   day: m t w t f s s

There are so many beautiful reasons to be happy

date: _____   day: m t w t f s s

SHIT I WANT

SHIT I NEED

FUCK FUCK FUCKITY FUCK TO.............

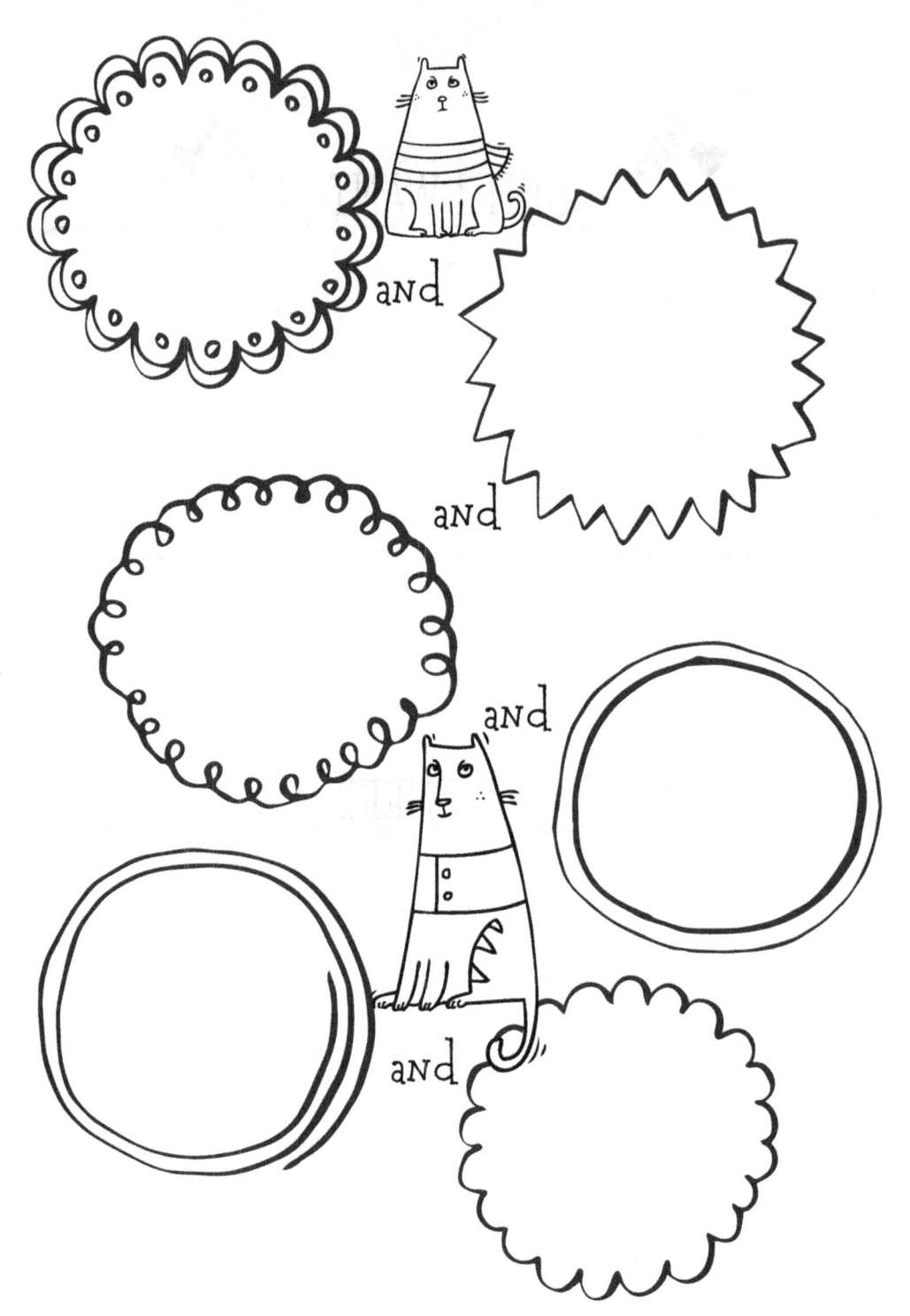

and

and

and

and

The Greatest Shit
I Accomplished This Week

date:_____

date: _____   day: m t w t f s s

Asshole of the Day

What I Wish I Had Said

I'm Lucky to Have

MY MOOD TODAY (Rated in cats)

SHIT TO DO

date: _____

Never GIVE up

SHIT I GOT DONE

PROUD OF

Random Shit

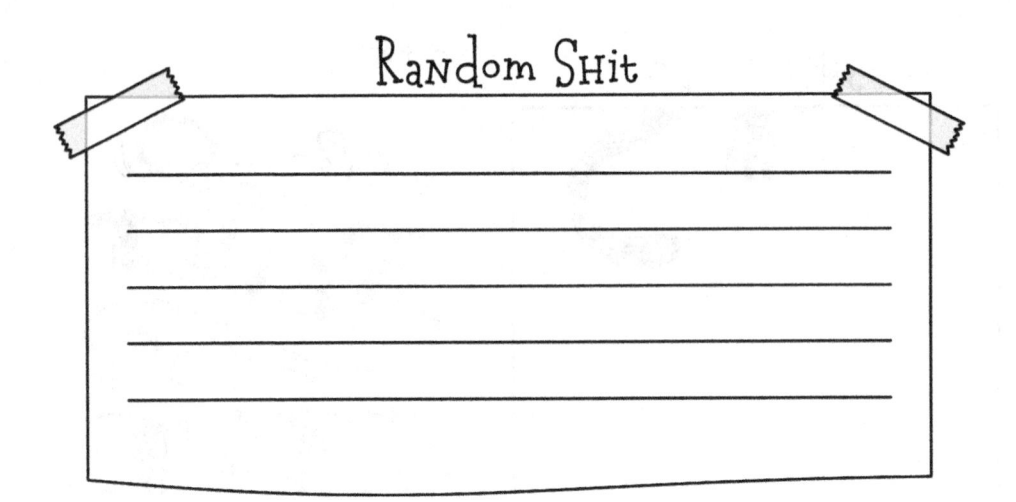

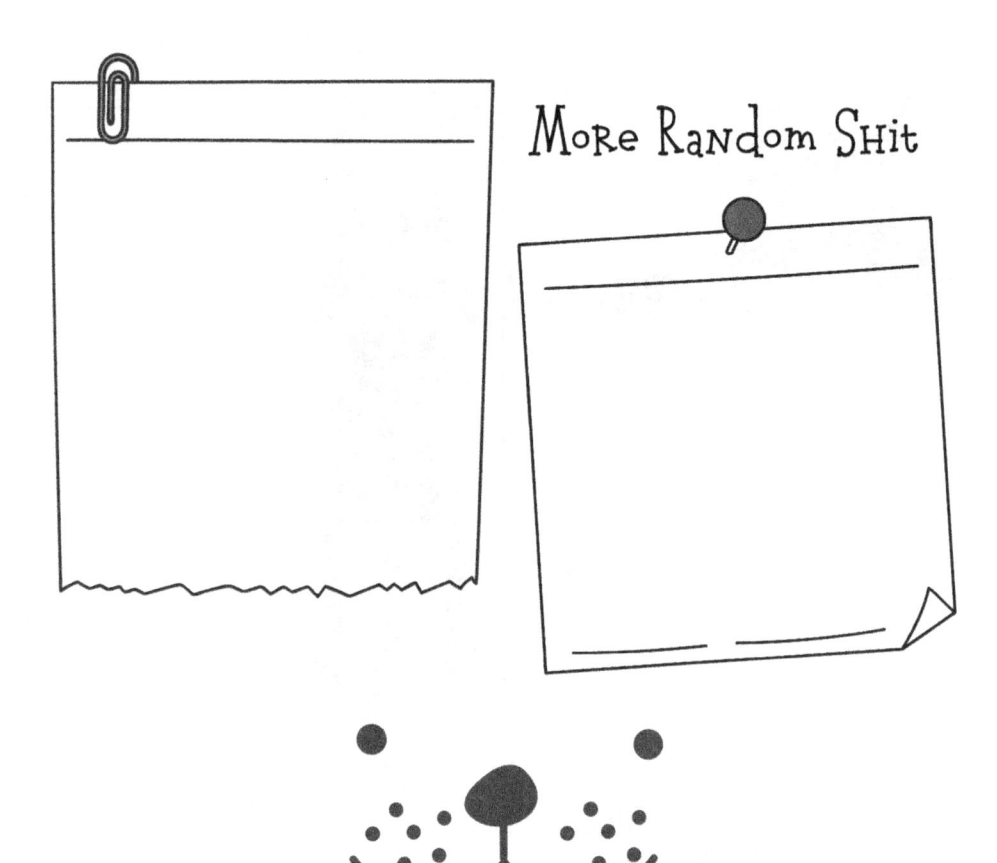

More Random Shit

date: _____   day: m t w t f s s

Shit List of the Day

Other Shit to Remember

difficult ROADS lead to beautiful destionations

CUSS WORDS OF THE DAY

date:_____ day: m t w t f s s

EXHALE THE bullshit

BULLSHIT OF THE DAY

date:_____   day: m t w t f s s

Life is an art
Paint your dreams

date: _____   day: m t w t f s s

SHIT I WANT

SHIT I NEED

FUCK FUCK FUCKITY FUCK TO..............

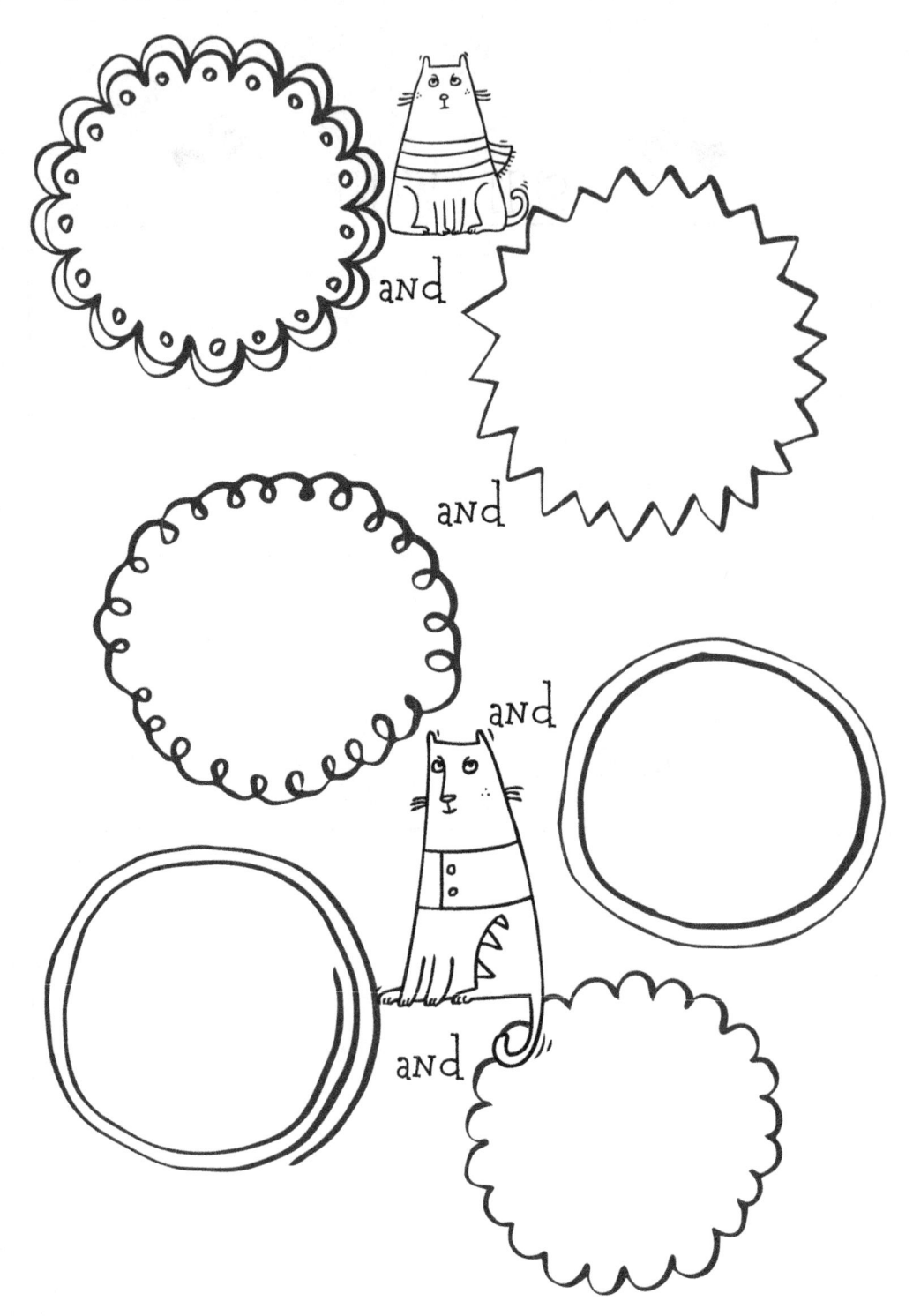

and

and

and

and

The Greatest Shit
I Accomplished This Week

date:_____

date: _____   day: m t w t f s s

Asshole of the Day

What I Wish I Had Said

I'm Lucky to Have

MY MOOD TODAY (rated in cats)

SHIT TO DO

date: _____

Love WHO YOU are

SHIT I GOT DONE

PROUD OF

Random Shit

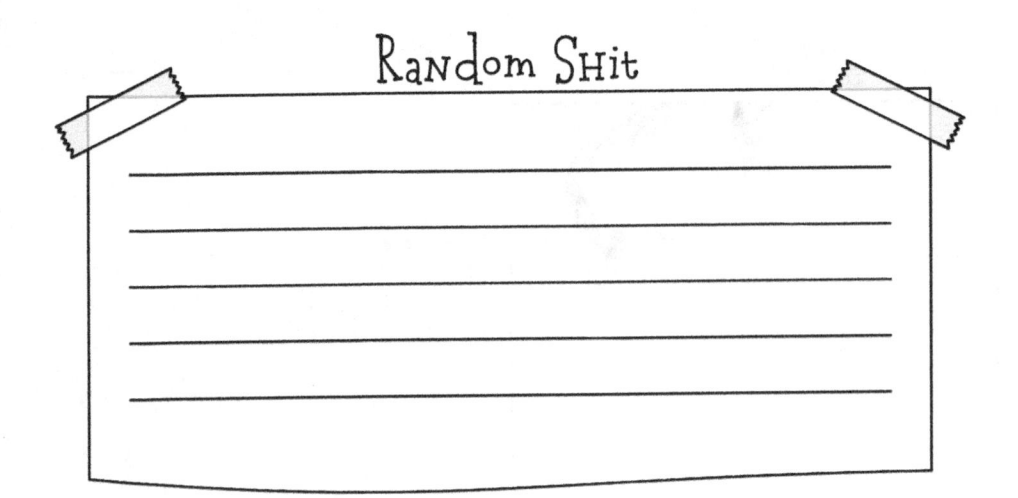

More Random Shit

date: _____   day: m t w t f s s

Shit List of the Day

Other Shit to Remember

The Journey is THE DESTINATION

CUSS WORDS OF THE DAY

date: _____   day: m t w t f s s

They **always**
get mad
when
you
are
finally done
with the bullshit.

Let 'em.

BULLSHIT OF THE DAY

date:_____   day: m t w t f s s

The Best View comes after the HARDEST climb

date: _____ day: m t w t f s s

SHIT I WANT

SHIT I NEED

FUCK FUCK FUCKITY FUCK TO..............

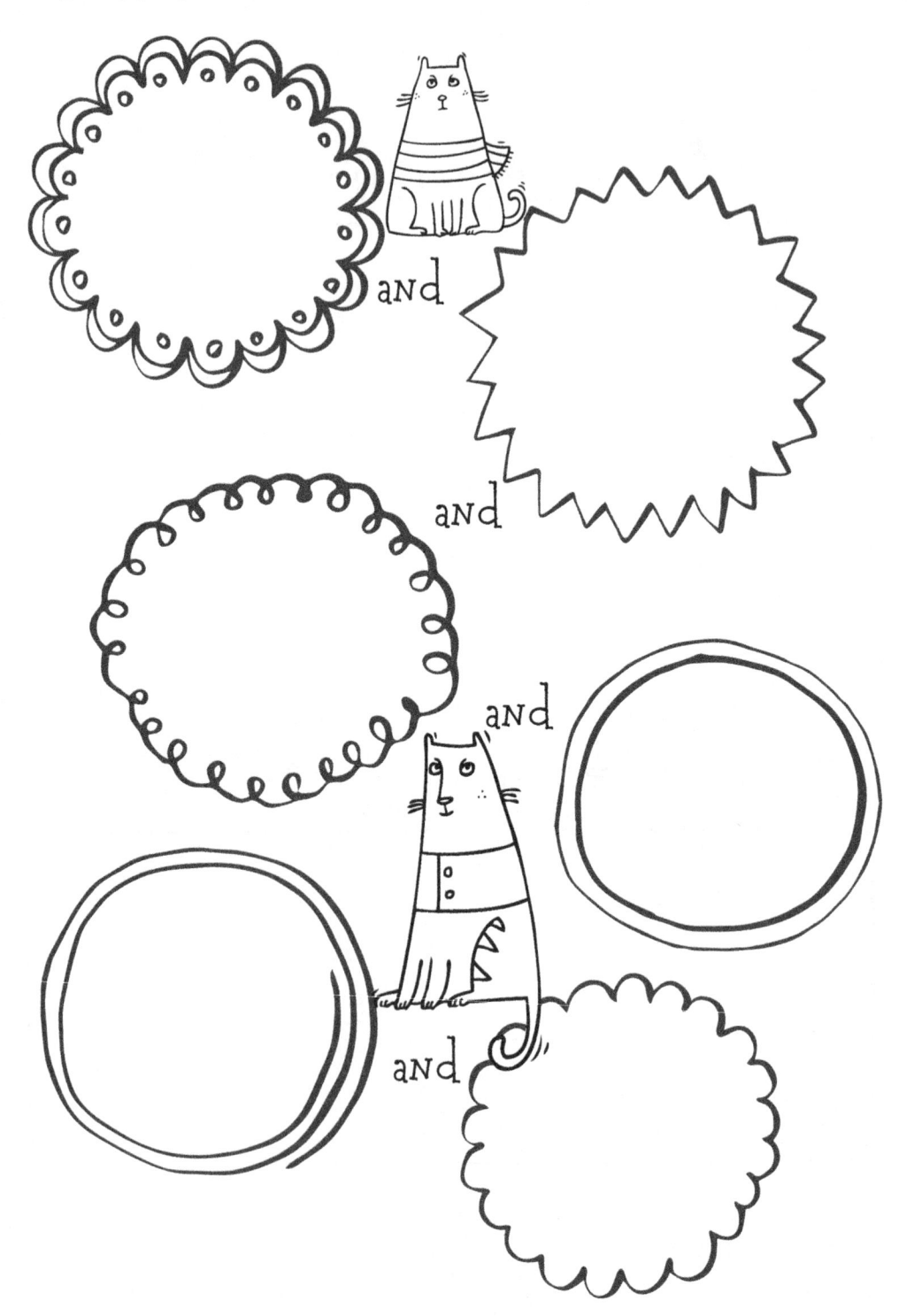

and

and

and

and

The Greatest Shit I Accomplished This Week

date:_____

date: _____   day: m t w t f s s

Asshole of the Day

What I Wish I Had Said

I'm Lucky to Have

MY MOOD TODAY (rated in cats)

SHIT TO DO

date: _____

The Best is yet to Come

SHIT I GOT DONE

PROUD OF

Random Shit

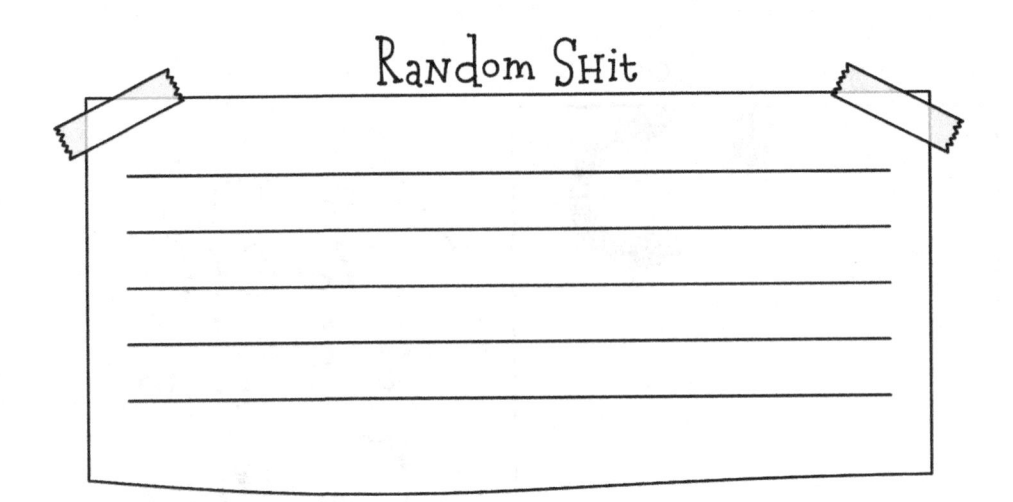

More Random Shit

date: _____   day: m t w t f s s

Shit List of the Day

Other Shit to Remember

all things are possible if you believe

CUSS WORDS OF THE DAY

date:_____   day: m t w t f s s

dealing with **BULLSHIT** is not for **PUSSIES!**

BULLSHIT OF THE DAY

date:_____   day: m t w t f s s

enjoy the small things

date: _____   day: m t w t f s s

SHIT I WANT

SHIT I NEED

FUCK FUCK FUCKITY FUCK TO..............

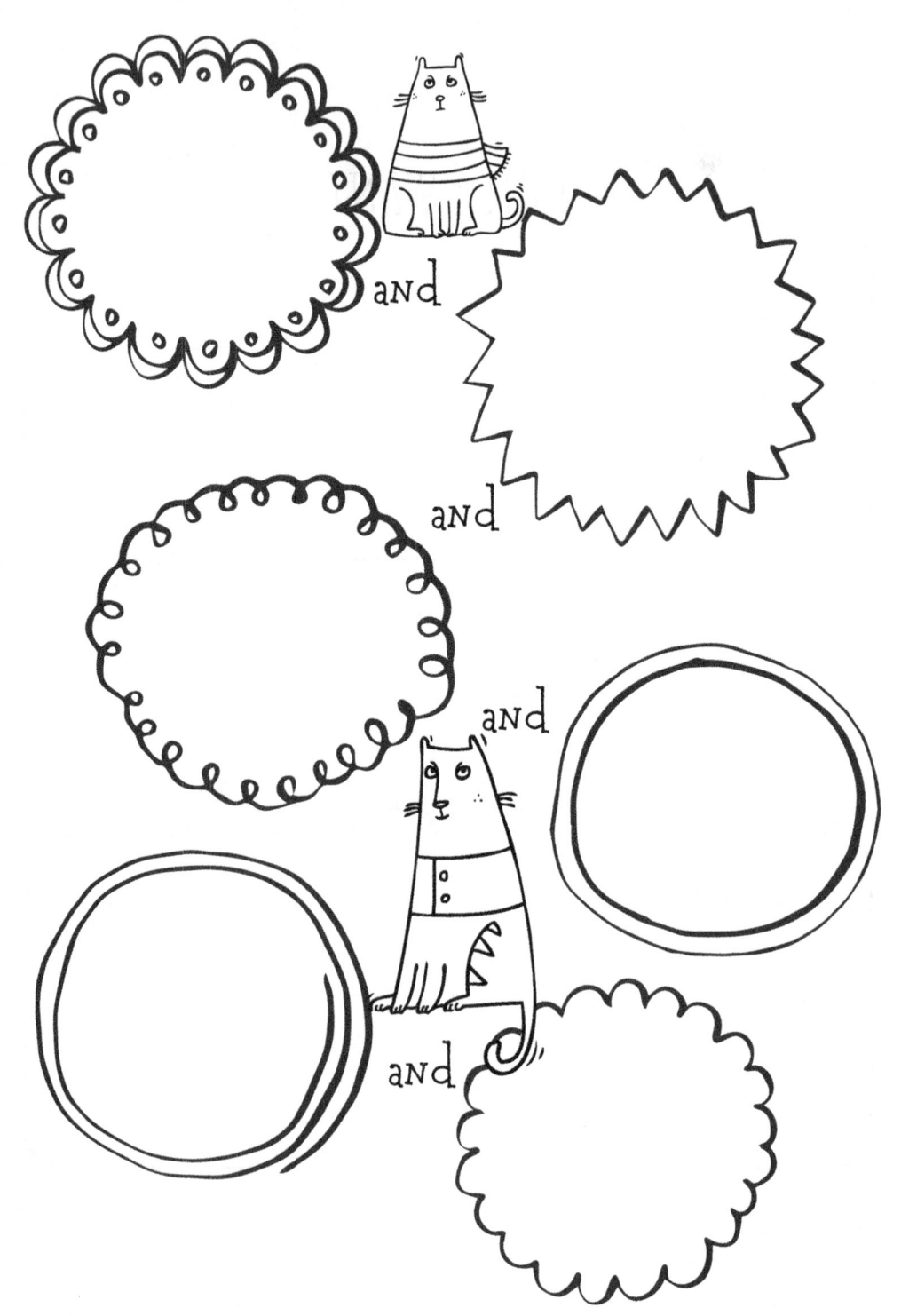

and

and

and

and

The Greatest Shit
I Accomplished This Week

date:_____

ONLY YOU can MAKE IT HAPPEN

SO GET OFF YOUR ASS AND DO SOMETHING!

Currently Happening in Life

MONTH: _____

LOVING	EATING	THINKING

GOING	MAKING	READING

HEARING	BUYING	CELEBRATING

SEEING	DOING	WEARING

date: _____ day: m t w t f s s

Asshole of the Day

What I Wish I Had Said

I'm Lucky to Have

MY MOOD TODAY (Rated in cats)

SHIT TO DO

date: _____

NEVER Forget WHO YOU ARE

SHIT I GOT DONE

PROUD OF

Random Shit

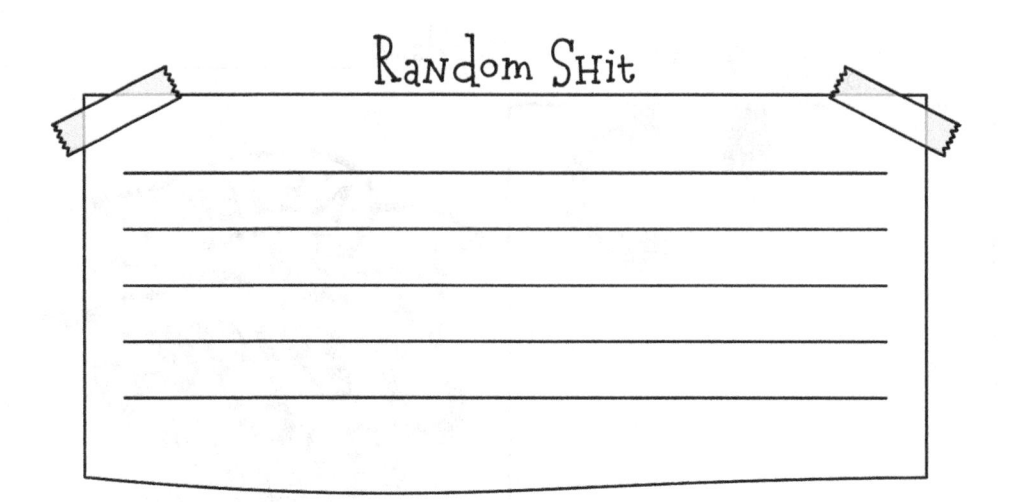

More Random Shit

date: _____ day: m t w t f s s

Shit List of the Day

Other Shit to Remember

life
is an
adventure
be an
explorer

CUSS WORDS OF THE DAY

date:_____   day: m t w t f s s

Expect the fucking bullshit but never accept it.

BULLSHIT OF THE DAY

date: _____   day: m t w t f s s

THE distance BEETWEN your DREAMS AND reality IS called ACTION.

date:_____   day: m t w t f s s

SHIT I WANT

SHIT I NEED

FUCK FUCK FUCKITY FUCK TO............

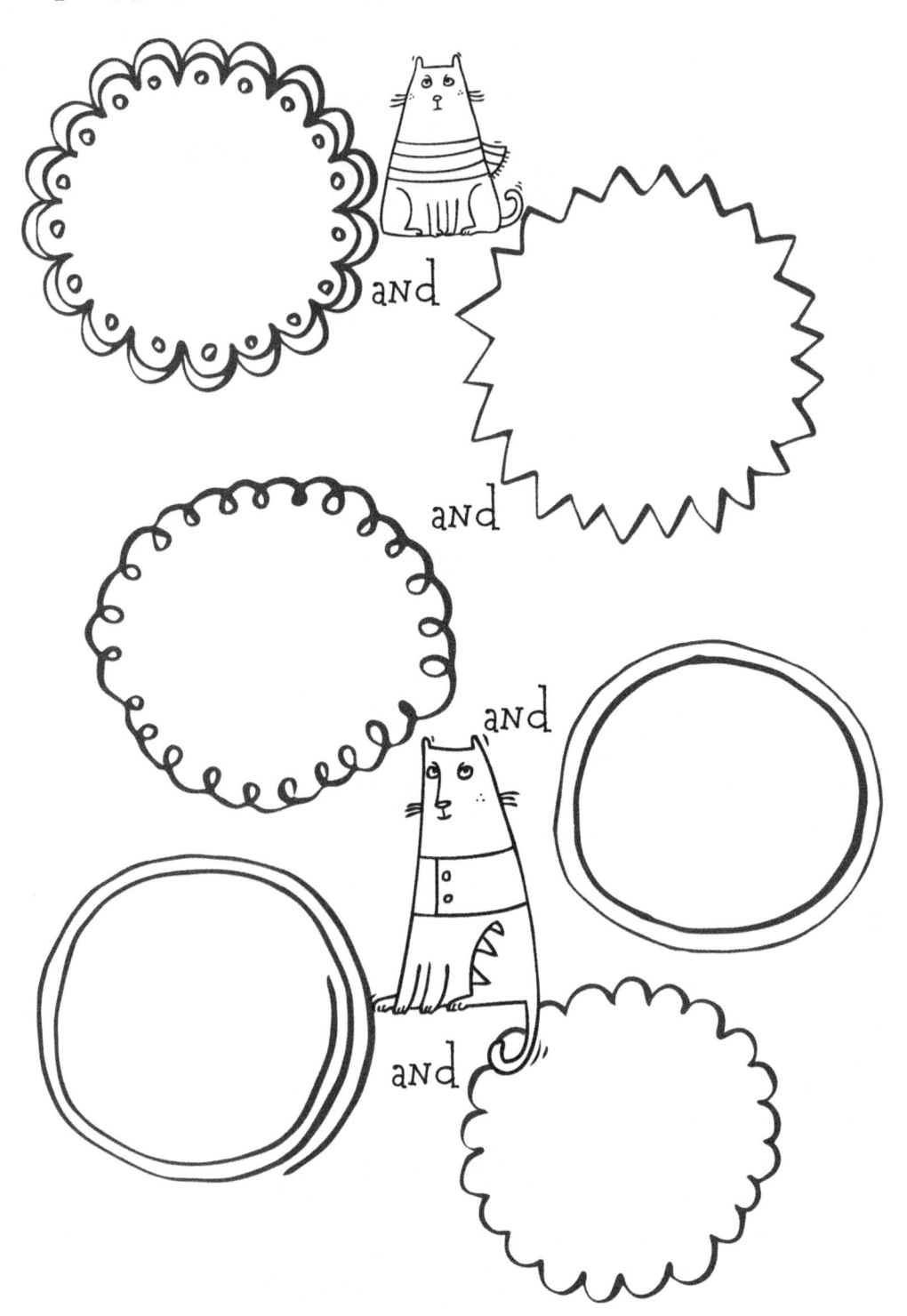

and

and

and

and

The Greatest Shit I Accomplished This Week

date:_____

date: _____   day: m t w t f s s

Asshole of the Day

What I Wish I Had Said

I'm Lucky to Have

MY MOOD TODAY (Rated in cats)

SHIT TO DO

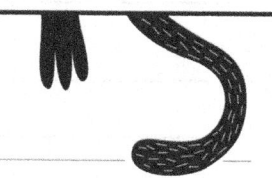

date: _____

Make Your Own Magic

SHIT I GOT DONE

PROUD OF

Random Shit

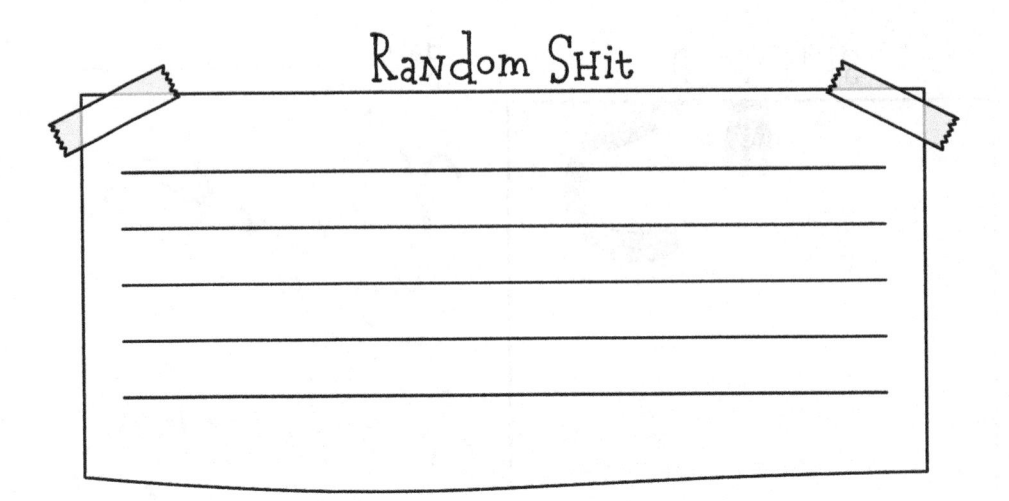

More Random Shit

date:_____   day: m t w t f s s

Shit List of the Day

Other Shit to Remember

Wake Up AND BE AWESOME

CUSS WORDS OF THE DAY

date:_____   day: m t w t f s s

LIFE
gets so much better when you cut the FUCKING negative bullshit out!

BULLSHIT OF THE DAY

date: _____   day: m t w t f s s

Use your smile to change the world. Don't let the world change your smile

date: _____   day: m t w t f s s

SHIT I WANT

SHIT I NEED

FUCK FUCK FUCKITY FUCK TO..............

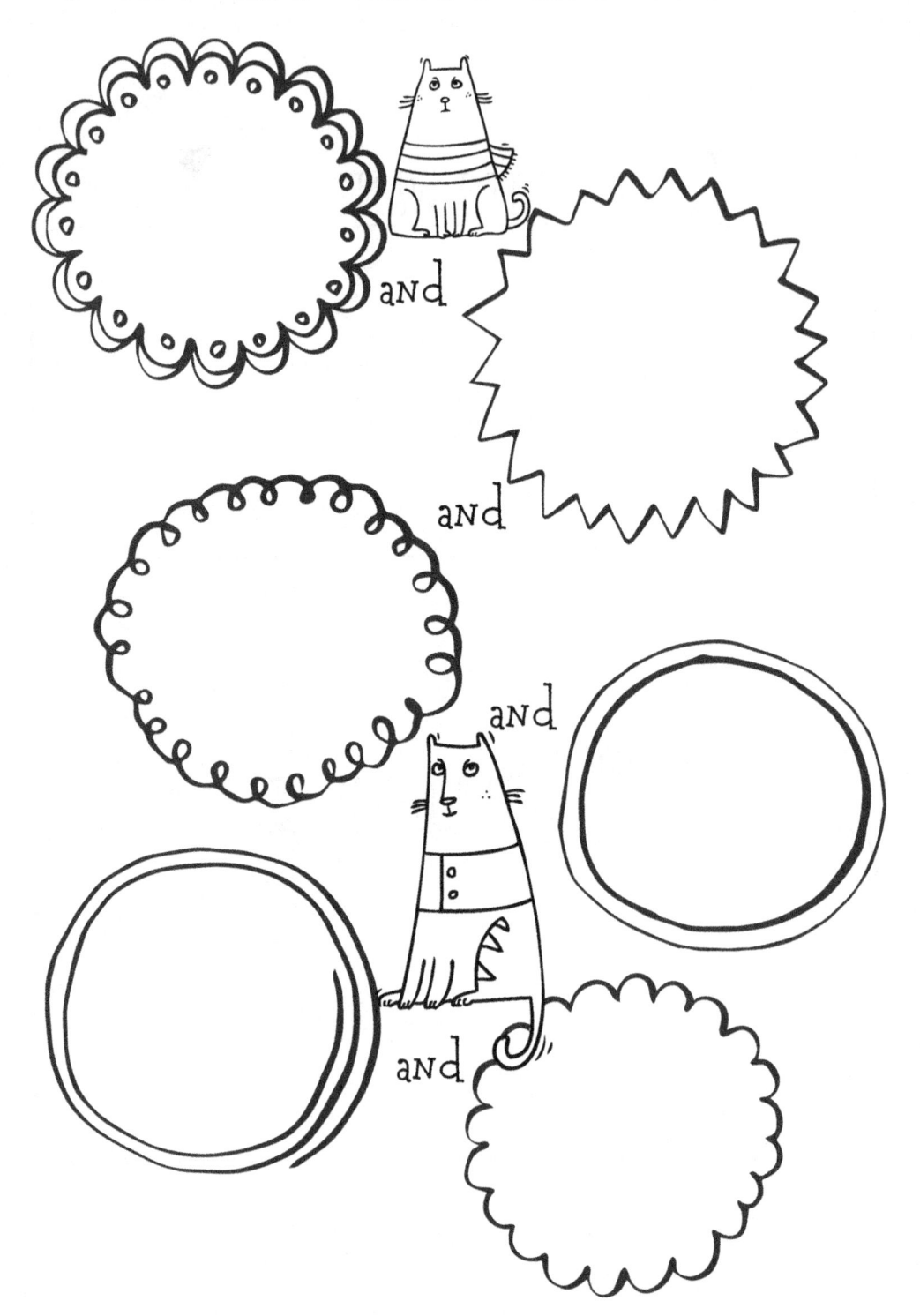

and

and

and

and

The Greatest Shit I Accomplished This Week

date:_____

date: _____   day: m t w t f s s

Asshole of the Day

What I Wish I Had Said

I'm Lucky to Have

MY MOOD TODAY (Rated in cats)

SHIT TO DO

date: _____

Live Laugh Love

SHIT I GOT DONE

PROUD OF

Random Shit

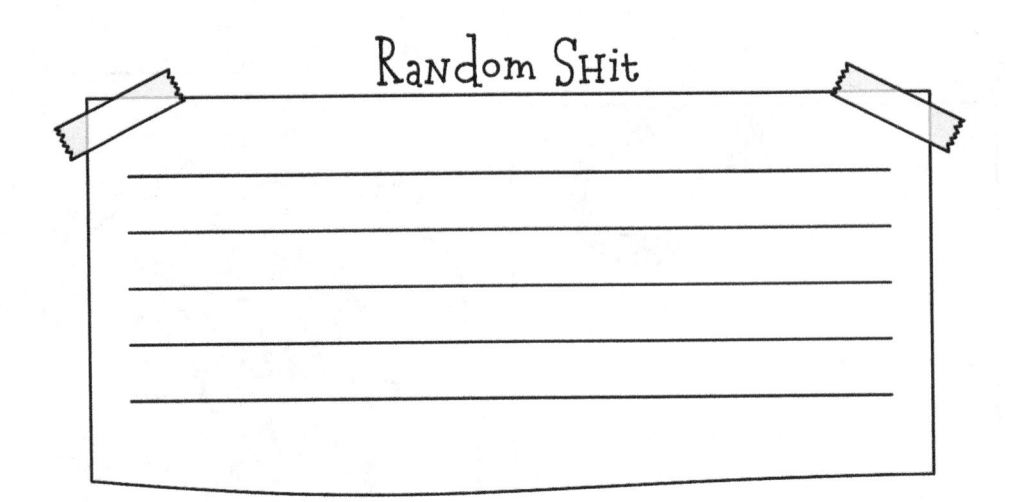

More Random Shit

date: _____   day: m t w t f s s

Shit List of the Day

Other Shit to Remember

Stop AND Smell THE Flowers

CUSS WORDS OF THE DAY

date:_____   day: m t w t f s s

EXHALE (THE) BULLSHIT

BULLSHIT OF THE DAY

date:_____   day: m t w t f s s

THERE'S *always* A REASON *to smile*

date: _____   day: m t w t f s s

SHIT I WANT

SHIT I NEED

FUCK FUCK FUCKITY FUCK TO..............

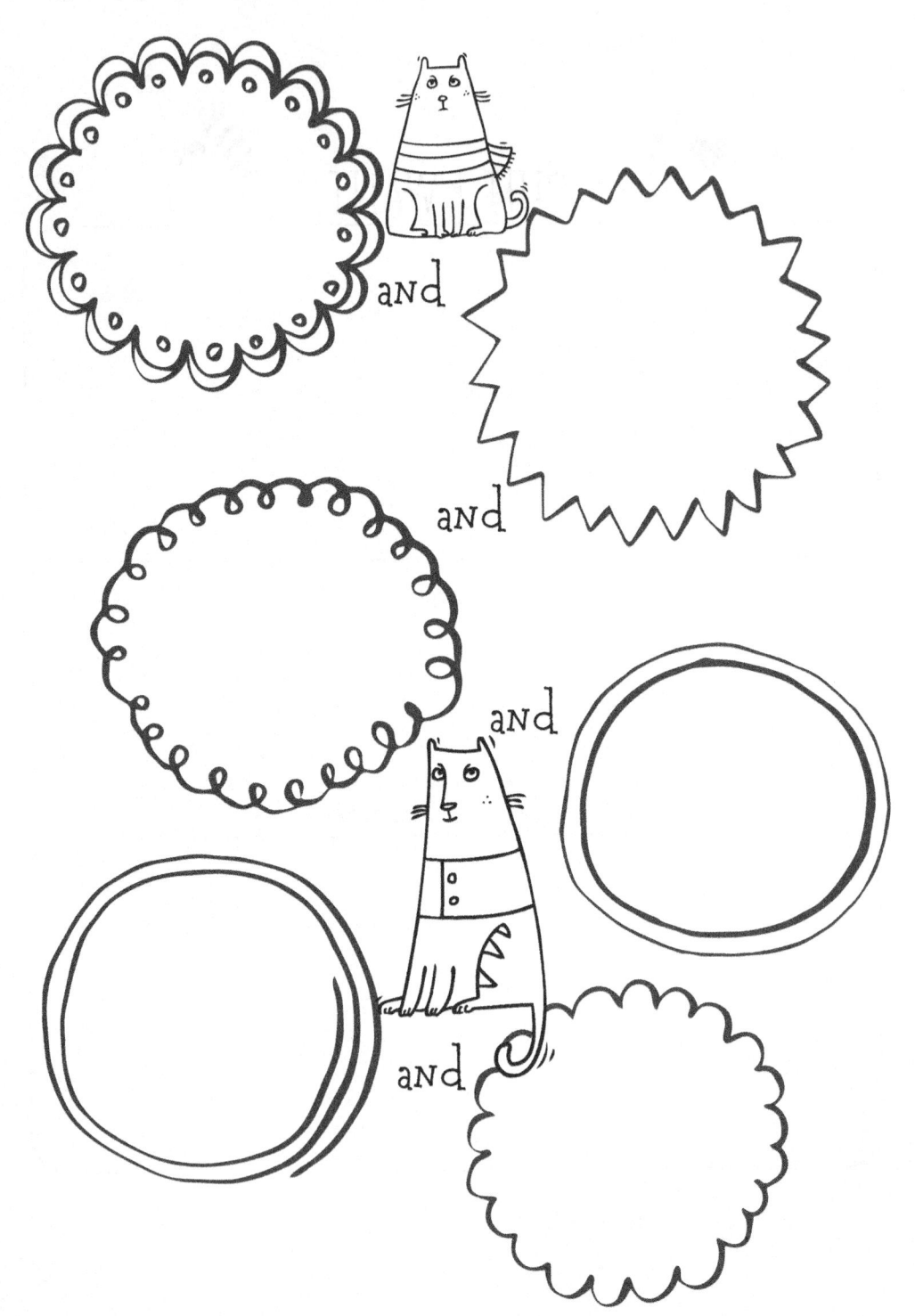

and

and

and

and

The Greatest Shit I Accomplished This Week

date:_____

date: _____ day: m t w t f s s

Asshole of the Day

What I Wish I Had Said

I'm Lucky to Have

MY MOOD TODAY (Rated in cats)

SHIT TO DO

date: _____

today is going to be a Great Day

SHIT I GOT DONE

PROUD OF

Random Shit

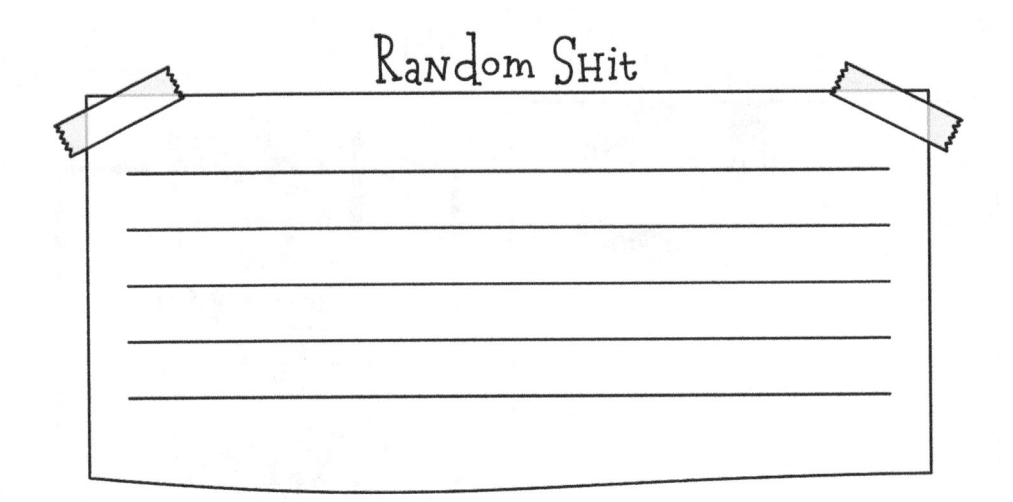

More Random Shit

date: _____   day: m t w t f s s

Shit List of the Day

Other Shit to Remember

Wake Up AND BE AWESOME

CUSS WORDS OF THE DAY

date: _____   day: m t w t f s s

Dear life,

I've had enough fucking bullshit to last quite a while.

Can we take a little break please?!

BULLSHIT OF THE DAY

date:_____   day: m t w t f s s

leave a little sparkle wherever you go

date: _____   day: m t w t f s s

SHIT I WANT

SHIT I NEED

FUCK FUCK FUCKITY FUCK TO............

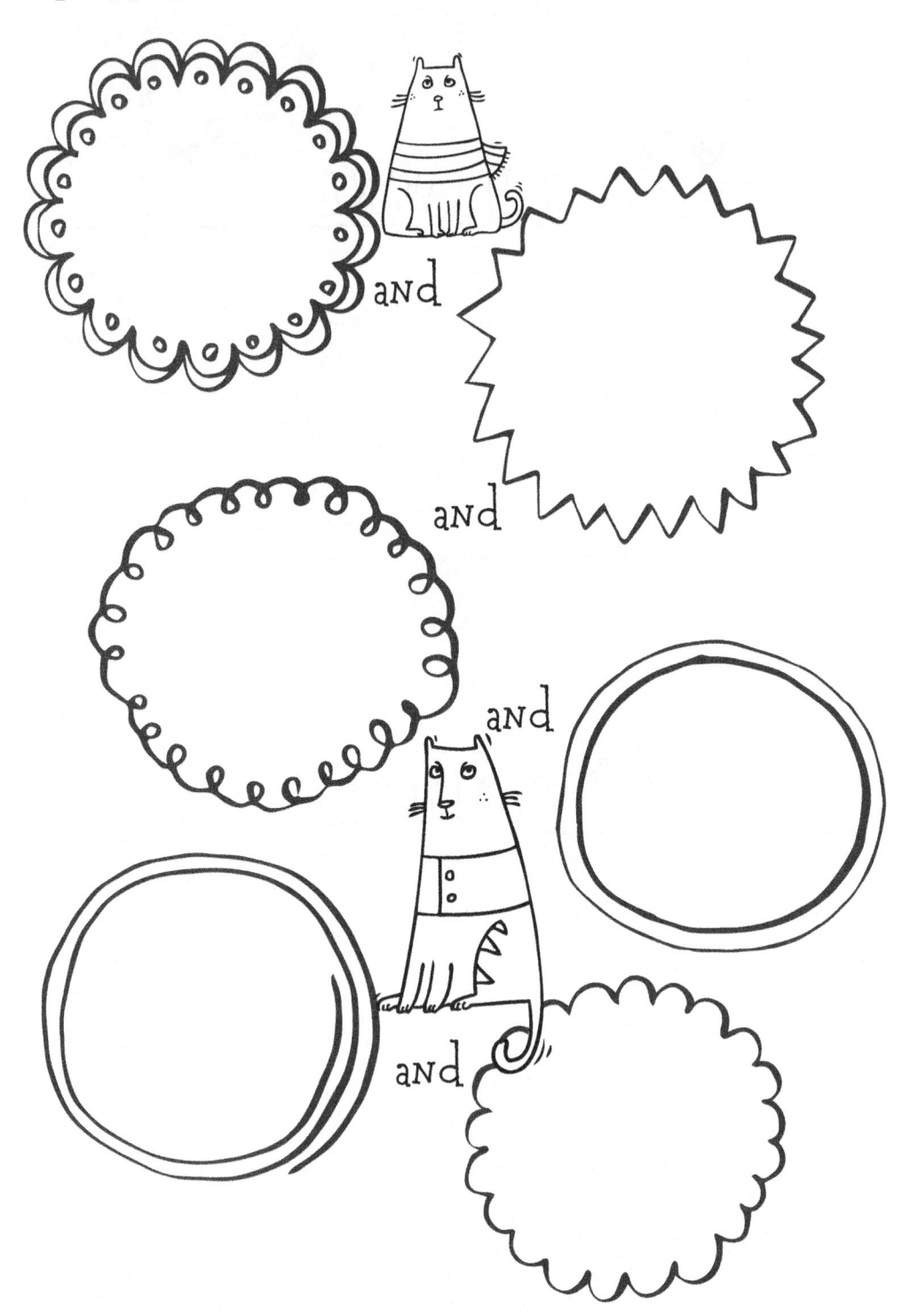

and

and

and

and

The Greatest Shit
I Accomplished This Week

date:_____

ONLY YOU can MAKE IT HAPPEN

SO GET OFF YOUR ASS AND DO SOMETHING!

Currently *Happening in Life*

MONTH: _____

LOVING	EATING	THINKING

GOING	MAKING	READING

HEARING	BUYING	CELEBRATING

SEEING	DOING	WEARING

date: _____ day: m t w t f s s

Asshole of the Day

What I Wish I Had Said

I'm Lucky to Have

MY MOOD TODAY (Rated in cats)

SHIT TO DO

date: _____

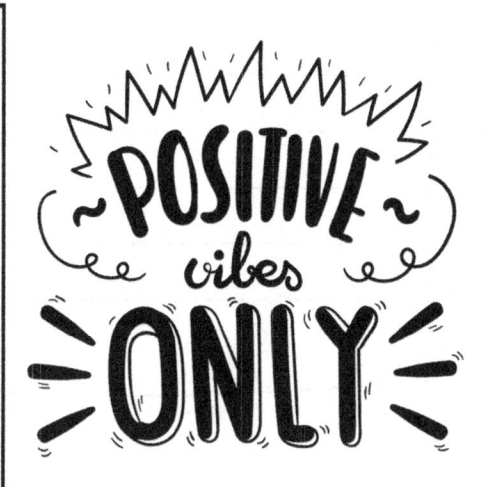

POSITIVE vibes ONLY

SHIT I GOT DONE

PROUD OF

Random Shit

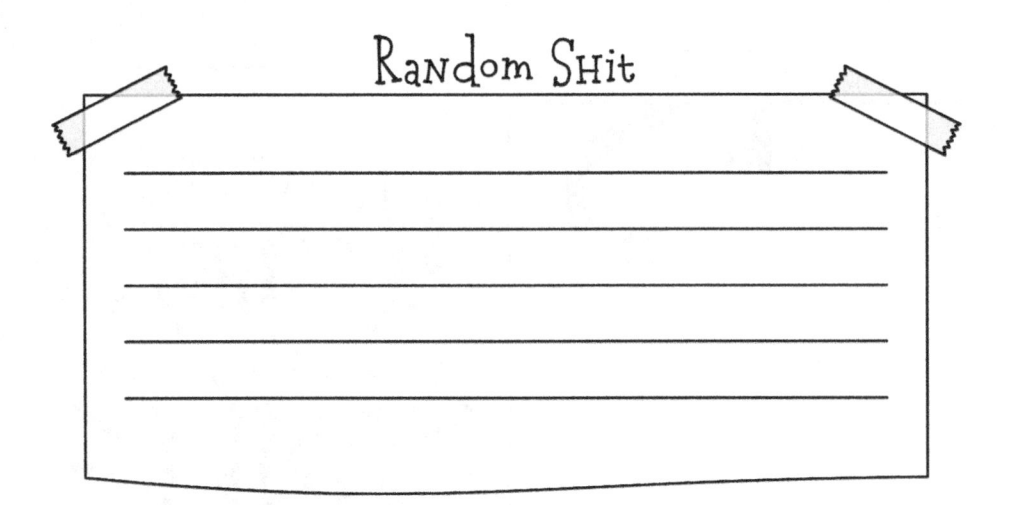

More Random Shit

date:_____   day: m t w t f s s

Shit List of the Day

Other Shit to Remember

make it happen. shock everyone

CUSS WORDS OF THE DAY

date:_____ day: m t w t f s s

KEEP CALM
and Exhale the fucking Bullshit.

BULLSHIT OF THE DAY

date:_____   day: m t w t f s s

Don't Wait Life Goes Faster Than You Think

date: _____   day: m t w t f s s

SHIT I WANT

SHIT I NEED

FUCK FUCK FUCKITY FUCK TO..............

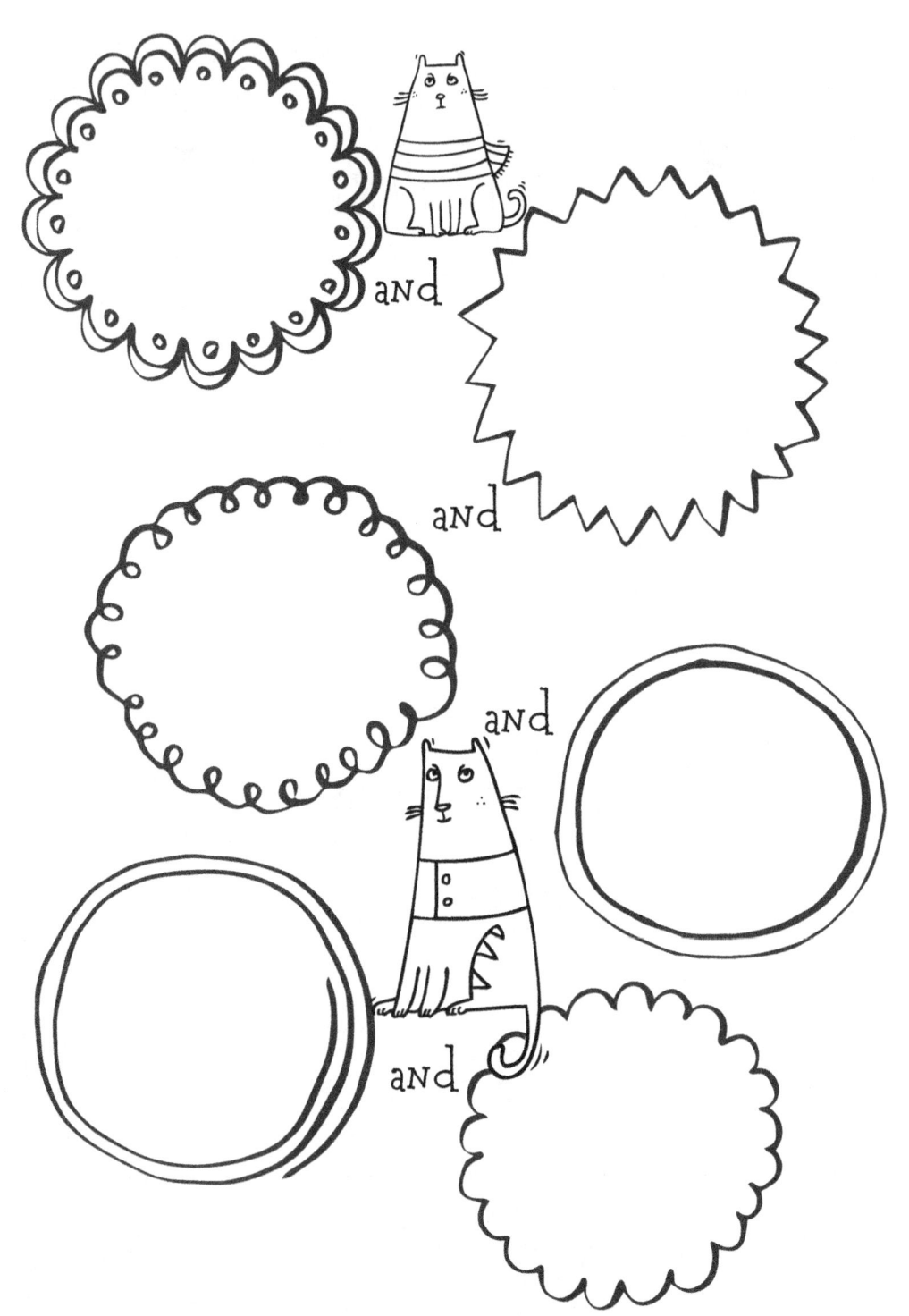

and

and

and

and

The Greatest Shit I Accomplished This Week

date:_____